> **Nature's Greatest Hits** <

Asia
World's Largest Continent

Joanne Mattern

Rigby®

Asia: World's Largest Continent
Copyright © 2001 by Rosen Book Works, Inc.

On Deck® Reading Libraries
Published by Rigby
1000 Hart Road
Barrington, IL 60010-2627
www.rigby.com

Book Design: Michael DeLisio
Text: Joanne Mattern
Photo Credits: Cover, pp. 4–5, 11, 21 © Viesti Collection; p. 6 (inset)
© Neil Beer/Corbis; pp. 8, 20 © Indexstock; pp. 9, 13, 15 (inset),
16–19 © International Stock; p. 10 © Roger Tidman/Corbis; p. 12
© Michael S. Yamashita/Corbis; pp. 14–15 © Dinodia

On Deck® is a trademark of Reed Elsevier Inc. registered
in the United States and/or other jurisdictions

06 05 04
10 9 8 7 6 5 4 3 2

Printed in China

ISBN 0-7635-7906-8

Contents

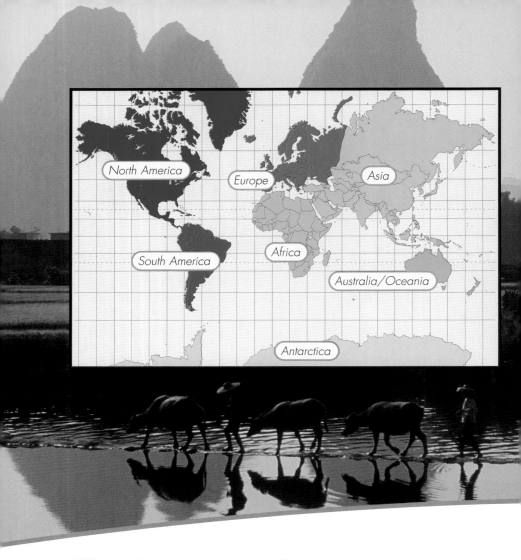

World's Largest Continent

There are seven continents on Earth. The largest continent is Asia. Asia makes up one-third of all the land in the world!

The World's Continents

Name	Square Miles
Asia	17,400,000 miles
Africa	11,700,000 miles
North America	9,400,000 miles
South America	6,900,000 miles
Antarctica	5,400,000 miles
Europe	3,800,000 miles
Australia/Oceania	3,300,000 miles

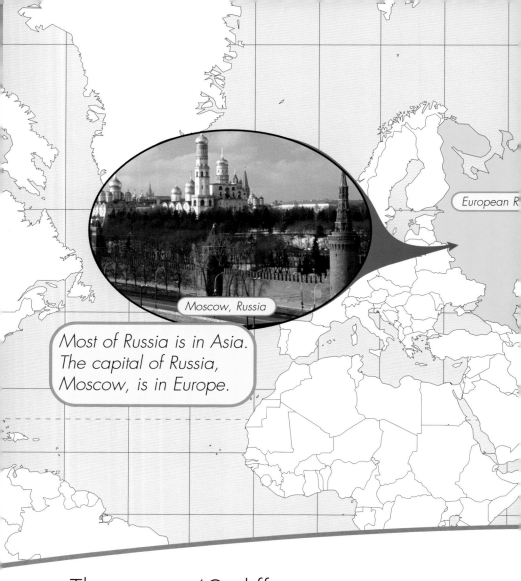

European R

Moscow, Russia

Most of Russia is in Asia. The capital of Russia, Moscow, is in Europe.

There are 49 different countries in Asia. The largest country is Russia. Russia covers more than 6,500,000 square miles. That is almost twice the size of the United States.

One of the smallest countries in Asia is Singapore. It is only 250 square miles. That is smaller than New York City.

Highs and Lows

There are more mountains in Asia than anywhere on Earth. Mount Everest is in a country called Nepal. It is the highest mountain in the world!

CHINA

NEPAL

Mount Everest

INDIA

Mount Everest is called the "roof of the world." It is five and one-half miles high.

The lowest place on Earth is also in Asia. It is the Dead Sea. The Dead Sea is in a part of Asia called the Middle East. Parts of the Dead Sea are 1,300 feet below sea level.

Weather

Asia has many different climates. The northern part of Asia is very cold. Parts of Russia are frozen all year long.

Some places in Asia are very hot. Rain forests in Malaysia are hot and humid all year.

IT'S A FACT: The oldest rain forest in the world is in Malaysia.

Plants

Different kinds of trees and plants grow in each part of Asia. Southeast Asia has nutmeg trees, rubber trees, and many other kinds of trees.

Rubber tree

Pine trees

In northern Asia, there are mostly
pine trees.

Animals

Many different animals live throughout Asia. People who live in central Asia raise cows, goats, camels, pigs, horses, and sheep.

These monkeys live in southern Asia.

People

More than 3.7 billion people live in Asia. Almost half of the people in Asia live in just two countries: China and India. Many people in Asia live in large, crowded cities.

IT'S A FACT: More than one billion people live in China.

Most people in Asia live outside of cities. Many people farm or raise animals. People in Asia grow foods such as rice or wheat for their families to eat. They also sell food to other people.

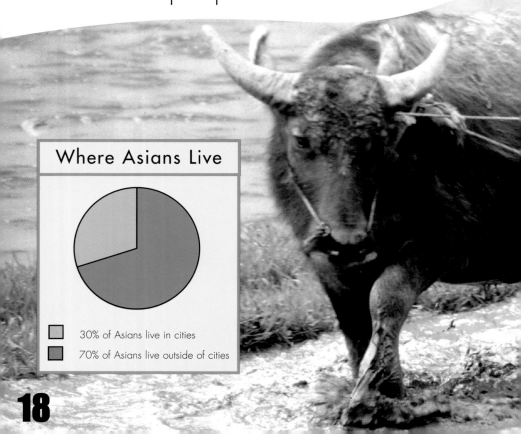

Where Asians Live

30% of Asians live in cities
70% of Asians live outside of cities

IT'S A FACT: The people of Asia grow more than 90 percent of all the rice in the world!

19

Asia is so big that each part is different from any other part. People in Asia speak many different languages, live in different kinds of houses, and dress differently from one another. Asia is the largest continent on Earth.

21

Glossary

climates (**kly**-mihts) the kinds of weather a place has

continent (**kahn**-tuh-nuhnt) one of the seven great masses of land on Earth

humid (**hyoo**-mihd) moist or damp

nutmeg (**nuht**-mehg) the hard, spicy seed of a tropical tree used to flavor food

rain forests (**rayn for**-ihsts) very thick forests that are in places with heavy rainfall throughout the year

sea level (**see lehv**-uhl) the height at the surface of the sea

Resources

Books

Asia (The Seven Continents)
by April Pulley Sayre
Twenty First Century Books (1999)

Asia
by David Petersen
Children's Press (1998)

Web Site

Asia Geographia
http://www.geographia.com/indx04.htm

Index